Why Stop at a Million?
The 10 Principles to a Successful Life

ALEX LEVETO

P.O. Box 3928 Alpharetta, GA 3002
ISBN 978-0-692-94238-3

CONTENTS

Principle 1: Life Is a Question Mark
    Why Are You Here? 1
    Passion...2
    Legacy 3

Principle 2: David and Goliath
    Believing You Are the One..5
    Rhino Skin 6
    Taking a Leap of Faith Even When It Looks Impossible................7
    Setting Goals 8

Principle 3: Circle of Influence
    Product of Your Five Closest Friends...........................10
    Find a Sensei..11
    The Alliance...12

Principle 4: Feed Your Mind
    Personal Development 14
    Affirmation: Everything Said Is a Blessing 15
    You Cannot Help Others Till You Help Yourself........17

Principle 5: Perception
    Polar Opposites...19
    Pointing Out the Positives in Every Situation............20

Principle 6: Be a Hustler, Not a Little Bitch

Work Ethic 23

The Process 24

Principle 7: Pray Your Heart Out

How to Stay Faithful throughout the Process 26

Thirty Minutes a Day Keeps the Ugly Away 27

Ticktock 28

Principle 8: Become a Walking, Talking Charity

The Law of Giving and Receiving 29

Fear of Loss 30

Impact 31

Principle 9: Freedom

The Pursuit of Freedom 32

Financial Freedom 33

Principle 10: Venturing into the Unknown

Comfort Zone 38

Conclusion 40

ACKNOWLEDGMENTS

A special thanks to my father and mother for raising me well. I appreciate their drive to be successful. They have shaped who I am. Thank you, Dad, for being my mentor during my teenage years and giving me an amazing opportunity to change billions of lives in real estate.

Thank you to all my online mentors, including Grant Cardone and Tai Lopez. You have changed my perspective on living.

Most importantly, I thank and acknowledge Jesus and God for getting me to this point and always keeping me motivated toward advancing to the next level in life.

PREFACE

In recent years, I have noticed a huge gap in the way people think. A chasm exists between the most successful people and average, middle-class people. This divide became apparent to me when I started hanging out with people who were at a level I never thought I could attain. They helped me see the massive impact a mindset can have on an individual's success. From those days to now, I have been obsessed with my success and helping others conquer their dreams and goals.

I grew up pretty average, going through the motions like every other kid. Today, at the time of this writing, I am twenty years old and glad I realized "what was going on" at such a young age. The infestation of average was all around me every day, and it took those people with incredible mindsets to make me aware of this. They woke me from a trance I'd had no idea I was in. Average anything is not a working formula. Erase it from your notebook, because it is no good.

In this book, I describe how I became the best me, and I hope this speaks to the person out there who wants to change their life in a positive way. I will present to you ten basic principles for success that have helped me reach another level in life at such a young age. The younger you are, the better position you are in to take advantage of *Why Stop at a Million?* and start applying these principles. You are on the verge of becoming someone great!

PRINCIPLE 1:

Life Is a Question Mark

Why Are You Here?

Have you ever pondered why you were put on Earth? Figuring out your purpose can be one of the longest journeys of your life. Purpose brings you a sense of accomplishment, and if you are truly good at something, do not be afraid to share it with the world. Growing up, most of us do not ponder why we are truly here. I never thought about my purpose until about age sixteen. Then I discovered a whole new world of contemplation about what it truly means to thrive and what it takes to reach success. I had discovered something amazing.

At sixteen, I joined a company that did not make me financially rich, but rich in my mindset—and this was priceless. I learned that someone can rob you of all your material possessions but can never steal your knowledge and experience. This mentality changed my life forever. This mindset was not ordinary. I discovered that my current place in life was a direct result of my actions, habits, and thoughts. The root of this new mindset came from hanging out with very successful people. This mindset was an achiever mentality. It helped me realize my purpose and why I am here.

It took me about two weeks of hard thought to figure out what I wanted to accomplish on Earth. A friend asked me, "If you could write your autobiography right now, would you be captivated enough to keep reading it?" That question hit me hard. We are never taught in school or in our childhood to chase our passions. Most of our parents will never tell us to do that because they want us to take the safe route. Before you scream at them, realize they want the best for you and are going to teach you what they know and believe and what their parents taught them.

The fundamental question about our life purpose should be one of the first ques-

1

tions we answer. Luckily for me, I realized my purpose when I was a teen because of some of the magic principles I will mention in this book. You might be asking, "Why should I listen to a kid talk about success?" I am glad you asked. Before we go into why you should keep reading this book, know that I am a land and lot real estate prodigy and expert in the Georgia market. You should listen to me because I did not let an age decide how successful I could be. Using all the principles in this book in real life, I have made more than one thousand big-money contacts in my first year of real estate, sold a lot of real estate, and helped a lot of people.

Once you decide to master the ten principles I describe in *Why Stop at a Million? The Ten Principles to a Successful Life*, you will become more successful than you ever thought possible. You can figure out your purpose if you just take the time to sit down and figure it out. With that said, what is your purpose?

SECTION GEMS:
1. Ponder your life purpose.
2. How can you change the world one day at a time?
3. What makes you unique?
4. Start as young as you can (start right now).

Passion

If you feel like you are stuck and cannot figure out what you want to do, ask yourself this: "If my financials were in perfect condition, what would I do every single day of my life?" It will take a few weeks to figure out what you want to commit to doing. Deciding what I wanted to do with my life took some time and hard thinking. One of my major concerns: Would I be good enough at my passion to be the best in the world at it? I have always set high standards for myself—something you should do as well. I was afraid I would commit to my passion, get two or three years down the road, and not see the results I wanted. That fear holds so many of us back from ever trying to go after what we want.

Recently, I attended a conference with more than twenty-four of the world's top speakers, including Les Brown, Daymond John, Grant Cardone, and Tim Storey. One of the huge takeaways from the event: I needed to stop overthinking my situation and just attack it and figure it out later. If you are not acting because you are afraid of something, stop letting fear paralyze you and just do it! Fully commit to your passion, and go after it with everything you have. Your dreams are yours for a reason. No one has your exact dreams. Do not try to be someone else. Be unique and follow your dreams, not someone else's. Leap toward your passion with any chance you get as early in life as you can. Do not base your future success on who you are now and where you are now. Taking your passion head-on is going to require that you make no excuses.

Through the day-to-day pursuit of your dream, you will learn more and more, evolve into a new person, and inch closer to achieving your full potential. Too many people give into others' opinions and are often persuaded to go with the safe and comfortable route or the route of chasing the other person's dream instead of their own. The safe route would be to go to school and get a degree to land a secure job and make fifty thousand dollars a year. This concept is so outdated. True freedom is doing something you love every single day and getting paid an amazing amount of money because you are so good at what you do.

I talk to so many college-aged kids every day, mostly because I am one. I ask them, "What is your passion?," and most of them do not know what to say. The next question I ask is, "What is your major, and what kind of job do you want to have?" Their answers always vary here, but the main response is, "I am going to become a _____ because it makes a lot of money." Everybody loves to make money, but not everybody's passion is to make money.

You should only be working for something if it is your passion. My passion is helping people and making money. Real estate allows me to do both. Regardless of my financial independence, I love the pursuit of making the next dollar while helping a landowner and homebuilder make a transaction. I also make it an obligation and top priority to reach my goals. If making money is your passion, I would expect you to not party all weekend but instead find ways to make money.

Passion should come naturally. You should feel a deep, burning desire to do what you love. Most nights, I cannot sleep because I am so excited to wake up and get back in the game. Do you see what I am getting at here? Passion is a major ingredient in the recipe of life because people tend to work harder for their passion rather than at a job they hate that pays a limited amount of money.

One thing I know about you without ever having met you is that you have greatness within you. You have a passion for something, but you must see that in yourself to become the person God has called you to be. Live a risky, on-the-edge kind of life. Stop being average. Be the hero of your own movie, and save the world. You only get one chance to live. The choice is up to you on how to do it. Decide to change the world with your passion, and stick with that decision till the day you die.

SECTION GEMS:

1. Chase your passion as soon as you can.

2. Purpose often correlates with passion.

3. If money was not an issue, what would you do every day?

Legacy

A legacy is built in a lifetime, not in a moment. Once you have figured out how to start your journey to become great by finding your purpose and passion, you must figure out what you want to leave behind after you die. Some of the greatest people on this planet are still remembered for what they did for society even though they have passed away. The best currency one can have is impact, inspiration, and love. You see, there is a lot more to life than just living in the present. Once you start to develop a successful mindset and drive for your full potential, you will see that your effort cannot only affect your life, but it can radiate from yours and change the lives of others around you even after you die.

Leaving a legacy of excellence is one of the best ways to change the paradigm of what people think is possible. This excellence involves being a master of every single trait I mention in this book. Go forward and make things happen because every second on Earth is an opportunity to provide not just for your family but for possibly the whole world if you truly believe in yourself and your cause. Declare right now that you want more in life, and obligate yourself to stick to that goal no matter what. Show the world that true happiness can happen from chasing your heart and working hard at your craft. Once you start pursuing your purpose and passion, people will follow you and your journey and become inspired by what you are doing. They will start to take action in their lives ALL BECAUSE OF YOU!

SECTION GEMS:

1. Leave a legacy. People will stay inspired by your life and actions.

2. The best currency one can have is impact, inspiration, and love.

3. Purpose and passion play big time into what you leave behind after you die.

4. Obligate yourself to leave a worldwide impact with your death. Make it significant. Go out with a bang!

PRINCIPLE 2:

David and Goliath

Believing You Are the One

When you start to understand your purpose on Earth, you may discover how tough it will be to chase your dreams. Most people will misread the effort and action you put into achieving your high goals. They have never experienced the struggle that exists between goals and the mind because they never set goals to begin with, and if they have, the goals were so low that they never got excited about their future. This lack of exciting goals makes people doubt their abilities as they move forward, and they hit some rough patches.

Becoming who you are supposed to be is not easy, and that is why many people have not reached their maximum potential or settle to live a comfortable, safe life. *The objective is not the hard part. It is your mindset that limits your abilities and belief that you have what it takes to accomplish and conquer that objective.* A major key to remember is that if you are not mentally strong, you will never be willing to endure the process to become a better you. Move past the negative self-talk thoughts and focus on where you are going and not where you come from.

All success starts in the mind. Look all around you! Every object was thought of at one time and created! Your belief in yourself comes from many sources. These sources include what you see in the mirror, your faith in God, validation of your abilities through your past actions, and how people interact with you.

Too many people place themselves around negative people and settle in groups that accept them for who they are in the present. People in these groups never strive to band together to get better. Instead, they hang out every night after work to spend all their money on drinks and fun. They live for the weekends. They also take awful advice and opinions from friends and family and create a self-image that is the opposite of what they were put on Earth to do. Too many people lack belief in themselves because they define themselves by their failures instead of simply learning from their failures and moving on. The biggest key to success is believing you are the one to change everything.

Rhino Skin

The term "Rhino skin" describes a man or woman who does not put up with any negativity and can always move forward no matter what people say about them. Rhino skin is also about believing that your why is stronger than your excuse for not wanting to complete something. So how do you get as tough as rhino skin? Fail more and beg for more rejection. That's right, you heard me: Fail. Keep failing until you understand that a temporary defeat does not mean you should believe you are a failure. For every criticism you get, use it to motivate you to push to become as tough as sandpaper.

Once you become supertough, no rejection will faze you. You will only turn rejection into another reason to reach your goals. Think of a racquetball game. When you are playing racquetball, think of your "rhino-skinned mind" as the wall. All the haters, all the excuses, all the bullshit self-talk, all the disbelief, and everything else you can think of lines up against the wall with rackets and bouncy racquetballs and fires away at you all day, every day on your journey to success.

Great people like Steve Jobs and Oprah Winfrey are not average. They pushed through all the discomfort and became moguls to be remembered forever. All great people rejected average and became great by using other people's criticism as a reason to keep going. To deflect all these sources of negativity, develop your mindset to become a fearless maniac who dreams to conquer every one of your goals and to ultimately reach your highest potential. Many people will see you hustle every day and try to slow you down with their input so they won't feel as bad about themselves. Once you develop an iron-minded mindset, however, people will see that you are on a mission to conquer the world and will admire you for your leadership traits and awareness of your inner calling.

Taking a Leap of Faith Even When It Looks Impossible

Taking your first step toward your goals and dreams might seem impossible because of the opposition around you. Many things will try to hold you back. Procrastination may set in for many people because of the "thinking" and "I feel like doing it tomorrow" kind of attitude. Let us say you have a job that you count on to support you, but one day you decide you want to start a new peanut butter company instead. This peanut butter business is not going to start itself, and it will only work as hard as you do in the beginning. You may have thoughts of leaving your job and going all out at your peanut butter business because it is exciting and new, but you fear not having an income and failing hardcore. You start to doubt yourself and your abilities.

Do not worry. This has happened to almost EVERY single person on Earth who has been through trials and tribulations to do whatever it takes to reach their dreams and goals. You have a choice. Either you quit now and continue to stay comfortable at your job, OR you can take a leap of FAITH toward your goals and dreams of having a successful peanut butter business. Of course, I would advise you to keep your job to keep producing income. That said, faith can assure you that God always has your back no matter what comes along and tries to knock you off course. You know as well as me that absolutely every amazing experience comes when you take a step outside of your comfort zone. For example, when you leap off a cliff into water for the first time, you get that special adrenaline feeling for a whole two seconds. That two seconds is breathtaking, and you start to freak out; but when you hit the water, everything is awesome and you want to do it again!

Have you ever gone up to a girl or guy you liked and flirted with them? If you have, it is the same experience with a usually good ending. Overthinking is a deadly killer of dreams. It is silent like an assassin. Act and worry about things later! Taking a leap of faith is the first major key to success because it will start you on your journey. Some people's leaps of faith are smaller than others. Everyone must get started somewhere, somehow.

Setting Goals

O nce you have decided to start your peanut butter company and leap in the right direction, you must draw a map to determine your destination. Setting goals is one of a leader's most important characteristics and highly determines how big one thinks. Most people set very low goals because of their lack of self-image and belief in their abilities. Another crucial part to your goals is to set deadlines. This will create a sense of urgency. If you have no goals, you will never know where you are going and will have no roadmap to show you how to get there. Time-incremented goals will help you gauge yourself on a daily, yearly, and five-year basis and are crucial to walking the path of success in any category of life.

1. Daily Example:
- *Have lunch with Karen*
- *Call 50 prospects today*
- *Film a video for my YouTube account*
- *One more hour of writing*
- *Read for 30 minutes*
- *Finish all my classes, Study for 1 hour*

2. Yearly Goals Example:
- *Close 50 sales this year*
- *Give 200 hours of my time, Give over $60,000 to charity*
- *Keep a strong relationship with someone*
- *Get straight A's in school both semesters*

3. Five-Year Goals
- *Become a better husband*
- *Inspire thousands of people*
- *Become a billionaire*
- *Give over $10,000,000*

Perks to Goals:

-You start to know your short- and long-term goals.
-You see where your mindset is.
-You get to ask yourself where you want to be.
-You get to observe and change priorities.

SECTION GEMS:

1. Goal setting is one of the largest success principles.
2. Set daily, yearly, and five-year goals.
3. Remind yourself of where you want to be all the time by writing down your goals consistently every day.

PRINCIPLE 3:
Circle of Influence

Product of Your Five Closest Friends

Now that you have set your goals and started to embark on your journey to your dreams, we will help you analyze your life in all categories. Principle Number Three is one of the most important steps to becoming successful: Who you hang out with, you become. If you are friends with weed smokers, you are probably a weed smoker. If you hang out with people who like to talk about cars, you probably like cars. If you hang out with billionaires, what are you? Answer that question. Look at all the great people in society. Who and what is influencing you? People are not your only influencers. The news, social media, your dog, experiences, and education all influence your decisions. Who do you think Ellen DeGeneres hangs out with, or Justin Bieber? Probably very successful people.

You are most likely as far in life as you are because of your five closest friends. Friends highly influence our mindset, motivation, ambition, and hustle. Your friends share a common activity, which in turn creates a feeling of likeness. People tend to get rejected by a group they aspire to be like, and they end up with friends who are accepting of them. When this happens, these people, in turn, settle for less.

I have learned that you must never be the smartest person in your group of friends. If you are, you probably should reevaluate your friends and reexamine your goals. Your new closest five friends should be the most ambitious, fearless people you have ever come across. Search for experts in the field you want to become an expert in. When you are starting to weed out friends, create a list of some of the people who should be on the cutting room floor. If you have been friends with Johnny your whole life, but Johnny does not want to hustle to get better at his craft every day, you cannot feed off each other's energy. No hard feelings, but cut him out of your life.

Removing someone from your life does not need to be harsh. You can still love that person, but you need to be straight up with them and let them know you are serious about committing to success and that you need encouragers and go-getters in your life. If you are committed to excellence, why not have a group of excellent friends? Work every part of your life to truly become who you are meant to be. Growing up with someone does not mean they should remain in your life for the long haul.

To create a life of excellence, start with a firm foundation of positivity and hustle. Every successful person has had a running partner and a circle of influence that helped them push to rapture in life. Now that you have your purpose and direction set, you need people in your life with the same mentality. It should be like an interviewing process. You are only looking for the best. Who and where are the people you want to be around? Most likely they will be hard to reach since they are well respected and busy. Once you start hanging out with people who want more in life, you will naturally start to want more too and will never be alone on your journey.

SECTION GEMS:

1. *Evaluate goals.*
2. *Evaluate friends.*
3. *Answer the questions, "Will these people help push me, and do they want more in life?"*
4. *Burn the old bridges with the old friends so you can never go back to hurt someone's feelings.*
5. *Make a list of the most ambitious, hungry friends and acquaintances you have.*
6. *Recruit the best.*
7. *Become a mastermind alliance.*

Find a Sensei

Mentors and teachers are going to be among your most powerful assets as you go forward. They will cut the learning process time in half because they already have the experience of chasing their dreams and finding success. In a mentor, look for the most experienced person who relates to what you are trying to do and schedule a meeting with them. They are likely very busy—successful people are—but plenty of them are waiting for hungry, ambitious youngsters to ask them for help. Successful people like to help other people! To secure a fantastic mentor, take them out to lunch or coffee and pick their minds for knowledge. Knowledge is 100 percent worth more than coffee. Who do they know? These people are typically well connected and know a lot of people in the industry. Try to set up weekly or monthly meetings with your mentor to catch up and seek guidance. To successfully convince a mentor to have coffee with you is very simple if you stay persistent.

How to secure a meeting with a mentor:
1. Find their number and call them.
2. Introduce yourself and explain what you do.
3. *Explain to them that you will not waste their time.*
4. Ask for 30 minutes of their time a month!
5. If you are lucky enough, you may be able to schedule a weekly meeting.
6. Have good questions for your mentor! Make the most out of both of your times!
7. Have money handy for coffee, breakfast, lunch, or dinner.

A mentor is not there to complain to about your life. He or she is there to teach you skills and to learn from. Ask a lot of questions while you have their ear. Bring your notepad and phone to add contacts that they may know who can help you. A good mentor will push you through difficulty to help you learn to be great at something. Meeting is not the only way to get a mentor. Mentors you respect can also be found online via YouTube videos or some other source of social media. You never have to meet them face to face, though face to face is preferred because communication is great as well as feedback.

SECTION GEMS:
1. Become a student of your mentor.
2. Speaking with a mentor for thirty minutes a month or a week will be great for your skills.
3. Take notes when you meet with your mentor.
4. Ask your mentor how he or she dealt with all the mental struggles of getting to where they wanted to be.
5. Ask your mentor what kind of principles changed their attitude toward success.

The Alliance

Now that you have created a team of powerful minds, you have unlocked one of the most crucial success tactics of all time: the alliance. From time to time, you should get together with all these friends and talk about ideas for inventions, new products, new ways to help improve one another, and just positive things in general. This will help you guys grow as a unit and spark creativity. Your alliance with them is one of the most crucial components to your success. Once you connect and operate as a unit, you can network through your shared contacts to meet successful people you do not already know.

Create this alliance to be around people who are adding value to your life and your mindset. This alliance should consist of people who have many skills so someone can teach about a subject that the rest of the group does not know. Try to keep this group to a limited number around five or so friends. Everyone must bring value to the group! The people and places you expose yourself to will form your perception of what is normal.

Like I explained earlier, you are the product of your five closest friends, as well as the environments you are in. That is why the alliance model is so powerful. These new success-minded people will have new ideas and value that will in-crease your success and knowledge of what it takes to be a hustler in every area of life. Everyone will add value not only to themselves but to each other. For example, I go to a book club every Tuesday night. This club is strictly dedicated to talking about books that relate to any area of life and how to increase produc-tivity. The overall synergy in the room is crazy. Everyone has a different input on the chapters, therefore everyone can benefit from others' ideas. This book club leads to great networking and gaining new ideas.

I also started an alliance group of the top five goal-chasing individuals in my life. We all agreed that investing and making money is something we all like to do and want to learn more about, so we meet once a week to increase each other's understanding of the different types of investing and how to do well in each category. Whether you go to a book club, get together the top five people you know and create the alliance.

SECTION GEMS:
1. *Get together a group of people who can help each other and talk about goals and ideas.*
2. *Synergy is a great energy source for hustle.*
3. *Place yourself around like-minded people if your mind is already focused on success.*
4. *If your mindset is not perfect, place yourself around people you want to be like*

PRINCIPLE 4:

Feed Your Mind

Personal Development

From a young age, I hated reading books because they were all mandatory reads for school. I had to memorize the content solely for the test. I was not interested in the true knowledge within the books. As I continue to grow and hustle my way to success, I have discovered that to succeed in life you must read books and always learn. Donald Trump, Warren Buffett, and all these billionaires make all the money not because of luck but because of their MIND-SETS. They are world champions in the field of personal development. Warren Buffett reads eight hours a day. He reads so much so that he can gain knowledge to consistently stay ahead of the competition.

Personal development does not just come in the form of books. It also comes in the form of audio, motivational videos, seminars, mentors, and plenty of other sources. Since the Internet has become such a big industry in the past decade, it has opened many educational platforms. Multiple people, like Tai Lopez, Mateusz M, and Greg O'Gallagher, have capitalized on this wave of personal development. Each of them specialize in different categories of it.

Tai Lopez specializes in living a lifestyle and educating people with knowledge from his book-a-day concept. He actually reads a book a day and takes all that information along with his lifestyle and shares it with the world through Snapchat, YouTube, Periscope, and many other sources. Mateusz M is very good at motivational films for YouTube. He creates multiple videos compiled from recent inspirational movies and pieces them into a montage with speakers such as Les Brown, Eric Thomas, and others talking in the background. People like him have created a whole market for inspirational videos on YouTube. I have recently come across Greg O'Gallagher and his YouTube channel. He creates content based around bodybuilding and his program, Kinobody. He looks to heavily inspire people through this program and help people with health.

Personal development has helped people band together and become a community of winners. It has allowed them to connect with some of the best minds in the world in order to grow their minds, bank accounts, strengthen their health, spiritual lives, and any other category you can think of.

Now that we can access mentors with the click of a button, you have no excuse for not having a personal development mentor. If you are saying you cannot find one, you are not trying hard enough. If you want to learn real estate, look it up. If you want to learn how to play guitar, check out lessons on YouTube.

I have used personal development a lot. I was particularly interested in a sport called Olympic weightlifting, but lesson costs were extremely high. The two movements in the sport are called the clean and jerk and the snatch. They were very hard to master, so I struggled through learning them without paying someone to teach me. My mentor was YouTube. It took time, but now I feel I have essentially mastered that sport. I personally developed my way to something that did not exist in me before. What can you use personal development for?

SECTION GEMS:
1. *Read more books.*
2. *Watch educational videos.*
3. *Get educated.*
4. *Stay on a consistent schedule for personal development.*

Affirmation: Everything Said Is a Blessing

Have you started talking to yourself in a positive way? Have you ever noticed how nice it feels? Then you've discovered the power of an affirmation. What is an affirmation? An affirmation is encouragement in any type of way you create, including talking to yourself in a kind way. One of the most important attributes to becoming successful at anything is positive self-talk. You must be your biggest supporter, other than God. The journey of success is long, and most of the time you will be extremely lonely. You must learn to thrive in this time alone. You are always around yourself, and you know yourself better than anyone else. By speaking positive words to yourself, you will see the potential of life and all its opportunities. Not only that, but affirmations will start to create a world of happiness for you.

Whenever you have a specific goal you want to hit, affirmations come in handy.

Let us say I take my goal of making a million dollars by December 31, 2018, and make affirmations for this goal. To get started, I would affirm in the past tense. This means you need to start acting like you have achieved your goal to convince yourself it will be reached. For example, I would say to myself, "I am so thankful that I made a million dollars last year." Most people think we are crossing the line when we talk to ourselves, but we are not. Ask these questions: Are these people who think I am crossing a line doing well in life? Are they where I want to be in life?

Another fantastic method of affirmation is imagining "it" happening. Closing your eyes and imagining the moment of success will draw that moment closer to you. Think of yourself as a farmer. You have your farm with all your seeds, farming equipment, and land. The land represents your mind. The land may lack in nutrition or may be very arable and thrive in nutrition. Every farmer knows that their crops will not grow in nonnutritious soil. Always start with arable land, or in other words, a mind that is open to new ideas and new seeds of greatness. The seeds represent your goals. How big do you want these plants to grow? Puny and lacking in fruit or giant and thriving in results? The answer is up to you. You are the only person who determines how big these plants will become.

Once you have started to plant your seeds, the test of time will do the rest, right? Wrong. The two vital things a seed needs are water and sunlight. Water represents love, and sunlight represents affirmation. Taking care of your seeds (your goals) by watering them with discipline and allowing them to grow in the sunlight will help them become giant plants that no one can tell to stop growing except you. After a good deal of time and action, you will be the best farmer with the best crops in all the land. Your mind is the biggest contributor to your success. You are where you are today solely because of your mindset. Change your mindset, change your world and future. Whatever you feed your mind, it will manifest eventually, so beware of the birds in your field of greatness as well as parasites killing your crops.

Affirmation can also come in the form of placing positive messages throughout your room or home. Take pieces of paper and write the top positive messages you can think of, then go around your room or home every morning and say them. Typically, I do this every morning because whatever you wake up to will usually dictate the way your day goes. Strive to be better than you were yesterday.

Another major key is to be extremely positive, no matter what anyone says to you. This especially helps in my real estate business. For example, if a prospect for a listing complains that the price is too high, the first thing I say to them is "GREAT!" The tactic here: If I am overwhelmingly positive in response to everything they say to me, then there is nothing that can ever be a fault in my eyes. My extremely positive perspective makes the buyer rethink the way he or she sees things. Everywhere we go, the world is engrossed in negativity. So many people complain without even knowing it. Become positive with everything you say, and you will see a whole new world of opportunity.

SECTION GEMS:

1. *Affirm to yourself that you are on the right path.*
2. *Become superpositive by always responding with positive comments!*
3. *You do not need someone else to tell you that you are on the right path.*
4. *Affirm yourself using messages in the form of writings and sayings.*

You Cannot Help Others Till You Help Yourself

To inspire others and help them become better people, you must become a better person. Everything starts with you and the way you think. Personal development, affirmation, and hard work will get you where you need to go mentally. You must commit to becoming a better person by reading and always learning. By always taking in good information, you add more expertise and value to your life as well as to others around you. Once you start learning new concepts and applying them, they will start radiating from you and people will be so curious as to why you are not "yourself" anymore.

Think about your phone, for example. People are always upgrading to the next technology to improve its features. Are you only updating your phone, or are you also upgrading yourself? What kind of software are you running on right now? Are you still stuck in your 2010 mindset, or are you thinking about the future with a 2020 mindset? How many years are you ahead of the game? Once you can start personally developing yourself, you can start helping others step up their mindsets as well. Going back to the chapter titled "Circle of Influence," the five closest friends you have largely dictate the way you think and how hard you are willing to work at personal development. If you are not already hanging out with people who think on the next level, you are most likely hanging out with people who do not care about their futures as much as you do.

If you are not putting yourself in a positive environment by choice, you are only hurting yourself. The only person to blame is you for all that you do. Once you make yourself better every day, you can start helping other people with some of the problems you have overcome. God has given you problems so that one day you may help another person with that same problem and change their life too. My greatest tip is to always have a thirst for knowledge. Learning will not only help you know more, it will also help you become more well-rounded. It only matters if you act with that knowledge in mind and help others.

SECTION GEMS:
1. *Always be learning.*
2. *Learn so you may help other people.*
3. *To change other people's lives, change yours first.*

PRINCIPLE 5:
Perception

Polar Opposites

Everything has a positive and negative side. Some examples are yin and yang, cold and hot, hard and soft, happy and angry. The law of opposites is a key fundamental in this universe. It is just as important as gravity is to Earth. It says there is a good and bad side to everything or an opposite view that can be perceived. Whether you think something is good or bad is solely up to you. Other people may perceive a rainy day as a bad thing, but you may perceive it as the best day of the week. To be truly happy, fill your life with positivity and see the good in everything.

Most people grow up with perceived ideas—in other words, prejudices. Once you choose to perceive everything as positive, you will enjoy life more than you currently do. Our "natural" reaction is to look for a negative in everything. We are hammered with information everywhere that everything is negative. A few examples of platforms that convince us that almost everything on Earth is evil are the news, some of the people in our lives, and social media. The news all day, every day, talks about murders, drugs, car accidents, world issues, and the list goes on and on. The news channels do not report good news because there is no money to be made from it. Cut out the news, and your life will be ten times better because you will not be consumed with the corrupt side of life.

Most people in our lives are negative most of the time. Generally, they are people we have grown up with. Sometimes the biggest naysayers are family members and your closest friends. Of course, you can change that once you grow up, meet more people, and start to understand your purpose. People tend to always want to talk about their problems and complain about something and put the blame on someone else, whether they notice they are doing that or not. So many people are caught up in always being around drama that they never pursue their dreams. If you have the right friends—they have great heads on their shoulders, are hungry for success, and do not put up with bullshit excuses—then you are on the right path. As I said earlier, be around people who are always doing better than you.

That leads us to social media. It has become an outlet for people to create an image of themselves. It has dominated this past decade and has a very large impact on the way we see the world. Once again, there is a good way to use social media and a bad way. A good way is to always empower people through your own personal brand. On the other hand, people abuse social media by putting others down on it or by overusing it. Overusing this tool wastes many people's most precious asset: time. Unless your business is social media, you should not be on it for more than thirty minutes to an hour a day.

When you are on social media, post pictures, articles, quotes, and videos of your craft that will build your brand. Choose the information you take in from social media as well. How are you perceiving things that are being said on this platform? Are you learning or helping others learn, or are you doing mindless shit that is going to do nothing for you but waste your priceless time? There is a lot more to life than social media and what others think about you. Every single person has a decision to make when it comes to perception. You can make it a bad thing in your mind or a good thing. The choice is up to you.

> **SECTION GEMS:**
> 1. *Your perception dictates how you see a situation.*
> 2. *Three leading factors of negativity:*
>   - *News*
>   - *Friends, Family*
>   - *Social Media*
> 3. *Train yourself to see the positive in everything.*
> 4. *Be mindful of what influences your behaviors and habits.*

Pointing Out the Positives in Every Situation

Can every situation be good? That question can only truly be answered by you and your paradigm. A paradigm, for those who do not know, is a way of thinking or a mindset. Whether you think something is good or bad is your choice. People will naturally want to be around you if you are always pointing out the positives. Unfortunately, not enough people point out the positives in others. People naturally put each other down to make themselves feel better. Everything can ALWAYS use more positivity. Lifting up each other and always pointing to the great things a person did will allow that person to open up and do an even better job. Everyone wants to be loved and noticed, so give people the attention they deserve and need.

But what if you're in a truly bad situation? Did your boyfriend or girlfriend just break up with you? Did your cat or dog just die? Did you just fail to make the cut for the biggest opportunity to go to the college or professional level of a sport? Your first reaction might be, "Why is this happening to me?" or "My life is over." Step back and breathe. God has a plan for you. What is the next step? That is all you can focus on for now. In each of these situations, the next step for everybody is to ask themselves how they can take something positive from their situation. Something "horrible" is happening to you because God needed that experience, person, or animal to transform you into a whole new person so that you could take the next step and become stronger willed.

We cannot always comprehend which way God wants us to go. Morphing into a new paradigm takes time, sometimes pain, and a lot of action. Regardless whether you are going through a breakup, death, or heartbreaking conclusion to your sports career, it was destined to happen to give you a reality check and to help you take your life to the next level. Someone else in the world is bound to encounter the same situation one day, and you will be there to help them get through it. This devastating situation may help you one day transform someone's life into a thing of beauty.

SECTION GEMS:

1. *Situations can be viewed from different perspectives.*
2. *How can you look at your situation in a positive light?*
3. *Heartbreaking situations can transform other people's lives.*

PRINCIPLE 6:
Be a Hustler, Not a Little Bitch

et us get one thing straight before we continue with this chapter: A little bitch is a person who whines or complains. Do not be a little bitch. Be a hustler. Stop whining and start working. I am sorry if that word offends you, but this book is a straight-up reality check on what it takes to be successful and let me be the first to tell you, it is not easy.

You might think, "This kid is twenty. How does he know what he's talking about?" As I mentioned at the start of this book, I began this journey when I was just sixteen years old. I developed my mindset and learned that hustling is a key fundamental for all who have done well in life, financially that is. Action is the key component to success. Reading, personal development, and networking are great and all, but they do nothing for you if you do not take the knowledge you have gleaned and use it. The only thing in life that people care about is results. Excuses are for the weak and for little bitches. The top entrepreneurs make split-second decisions instead of putting something off for hours, days, weeks, or years.

The number 95 stands for the hours a week you should be hustling your ass off to accomplish your purpose. The only person getting in the way of your success is you. No other person is to blame. Sometimes you will feel like giving up, and sometimes you will win beyond belief. Winning is one of the less-traveled routes. Frankly, it is so difficult to get on that path because it is made out to be something different than the path of failures and defeats. The road of failures and defeats is the whole first part of the road trip to success. I know this well. I started selling real estate in July 2015 and did not get paid a cent until exactly one year and one month later.

People, success takes time. It will not come to you with the snap of your fingers, but your work will pay off. My best friend, Harrison Nevel, began pursuing his passion—giving great fashion advice on YouTube—in January 2016. As of this writing, almost a year and a half and a lot of hard work have passed, and his subscriber count has jumped from zero to 90,500! Harrison strives to inspire others to help them attain great fashion sense. For him, it is not about the money. It is about passion and creativity. Look him up on YouTube. Passion, purpose, knowledge, and creativity are some of the key reasons why Harrison is doing so well.

Do you truly think success will come to you without doing the work? People almost always quit on the road to maximum success because they do not have passion, do not see results, or are very satisfied with where they are. Do not be that person. Do not be average. The wealthy have done far more than the average person. They have not only worked their ass off to get where they are, but all of them—athletes, CEOs, actors and more—have shown action through a consistent schedule even after reaching the top of the ladder.

Regardless whether you want these top earners to win in real life, you must respect the effort they have put in to get to where they are. How many downfalls did they have? How long did it take them to reach the pinnacle of success? How many hours did they put in a day? Is there a secret to their success?

SECTION GEMS:

1. *The secret to success: Work your ass off at something you enjoy and that pays or will pay phenomenally well.*
2. *Stop being a whiner and start being a producer.*
3. *DO NOT SETTLE. DO NOT BE AVERAGE.*
4. *Work harder than anyone else.*
5. *Do not quit when you do not see results if know you are doing the right things.*

Work Ethic

Work ethic can be trained. You can train and train until you die. The longer you can stand to work, the better. Hopefully this "work" is toward your passion and not just toward a paycheck. Fact is, most people have average or horrible work ethics. A lot of people quit after a short time to take breaks. But success is not waiting for you. Success only attracts great people with great work ethics—people who perform the right activities consistently. The more you work toward your goals, the better shot you have at achieving them. There is always another person who is trying to be better at your craft. Let that drive you. The more you slack off, the more time the opponent is putting in. You are the creator of your journey and the degree of your result! Working can become fun if you love what you do. If you work every day toward something you already love, your work ethic will naturally last a lot longer because you will not have to push yourself to keep going.

Sometimes, you will not want to work. Almost everybody will tell you that breaks are necessary and are fine to take. Just remember that every second you take away from your focus, another person is fighting to achieve the same thing as you. If you dream to build the largest real estate firm on Earth, become a Nike athlete, start a luxury-clothing brand, or own a private jet, they all require the same thing: a sickening work ethic. Family members and friends are going to tell you to slow down and take a break. From my own experience, I can tell you that people will always attempt to slow you down. The average person does not understand the concept of success and the effort and principles involved.

People will always try to slow you down because they feel uneasy when you are operating at a higher level than they are. People want you to slow down so that they can feel better about their lack of action. That is why you must hang out with people who are at a higher level than you. This is crucial. Do not give in to the pressure of fitting in. The feeling of acceptance is one of the best feelings any human can have. However, to succeed, you must break out of the herd mentality and create your own path. Do not get caught up in what everyone else is doing without thinking twice of where you will end up in the future. Take smart action!

SECTION GEMS:
1. *Train your work ethic.*
2. *What is your maximum potential for your work ethic?*
3. *Work smart. This is crucial.*

The Process

The process is the foundation to success. The person you will become through the process of struggle, pain, highs and lows, not being paid for long periods of time, and self-doubt will shape you into a whole new person. This will bring you closer to your goals. This "new you" will be much tougher and willing to take on a lot more. Do you want to stay at your current level for the rest of your life, or do you want to keep on moving forward and create a legacy for you and your family?

The process is not easy. It is the most difficult and long journey you will ever embark on. There are NO SHORTCUTS. So many people always look for the easy way out and will never do whatever it takes to succeed. People do find the easy way out: They quit. Barely anyone has reached the limelight because so many people try to cheat their way through the process of becoming successful. Every successful person's secret to their abundance is hard work performed diligently and consistently over a long time. Every day, you must hammer out stuff that needs to be done that no one else wants to do. Think of things that no one has executed so far in life, and dominate that space. The process of becoming someone great comes with no excuses and no days off. You will learn to thrive in your space and new environment.

Choose a craft that you love to work at regardless whether you would make money at it or not. If you grind at something you already love, the process will be ten times easier. The process requires you to get outside of your comfort zone and attack the things you felt uncomfortable about before. For example, when I started in real estate, I was scared to pick up the phone and make cold calls. Cold calls are crucial to my business to secure new leads. I would delay the calls to avoid my fear of the unknown.

One day, I decided that the only way to get results was to make the calls and contact strangers because that was where the money was sitting and it was the zone where most people would not dare to go. Today, I am not afraid to call a random prospect about their property because a) I know I can help them with a service, b) I know I can execute and sell their property, c) I know I am a confident person, and d) I know that no one else can make calls like I can. The process has changed me into a brand-new creature with a mindset that is always thirsty for knowledge. Figure out what process it takes for you to reach your success.

SECTION GEMS:
1. *Learn to thrive in the process.*
2. *Dominate the areas others scurry away from.*
3. *Choose a craft you love.*
4. *No days off.*

PRINCIPLE 7:
Pray Your Heart Out

How to Stay Faithful throughout the Process

To keep pursuing your dream, you must connect with your creator to clearly understand the defined path your god has intended for you. Whoever your higher power is, pray to that spirit every day and thrive off that positive energy. Throughout the process of defeat after defeat and small daily victories, you will need to stay faithful and believe that you are destined for greatness only if you take the steps your creator puts in front of you. Set aside time each day to worship your creator and ask him for help.

Sometimes you will want to quit, but know that a greater purpose exists for you on the other side of temporary defeat. Your creator has set aside a spot for you to be successful and to reach your goals. Thrive in the fact that you are destined for greatness and that temporary defeat is only your choice to let it defeat you. There is another power at play that is higher than a human's comprehension. This is one power you must learn to connect with to enhance your results. On another level, if you are trying to pursue a religious career, this is all too familiar to you. You know that to become a better speaker and to change people's spiritual lives, you must connect with God every day and ask for guidance and help to become better.

The supernatural force loves to know that deep down you are putting your faith in it to perform miracles for you. In my life, I follow Christ. On my journey to success, I have dwelled in Christ and put my faith in him and I have seen amazing things happen. There have been some serious times when I felt like I was stuck in a ditch and then suddenly, I was hit with an opportunity. One day in real estate, you feel like you have nothing to do and then you wake up after a night of praying and have so much stuff to do you almost cannot do it all. Christ has helped me realize my purpose, why I should be obligated for success, and that my dreams are mine for a reason and are not an accident. This has led me to see that when the bills come, I am paying with what I have put into my work and

26

not with others' opinions of my dreams. The positive energy of Christ's life and spirit help me know that every situation, downfall, and victory are for a reason. Christ allows me to have courage and confidence to go forward in any situation and dominate in God's name.

SECTION GEMS:
1. *Maintain faith that you are destined for greatness.*
2. *Connect with your creator.*
3. *Ask for guidance.*

Thirty Minutes a Day Keeps the Ugly Away

Since you have decided to pursue a relationship with your creator, make time for him. Every morning, every night, every day, take thirty measly minutes to center your focus on worshipping, putting full faith in, and learning more about your creator. I hope you will start to look forward to this time and center yourself around positive energy. This process will help you get on a better emotional level and start your days with riveting concentration and motivation.

I tend to start my days with a daily devotional followed by praying to God for guidance for the day. This simple thirty-minute routine reminds me that I have a higher power on my side and that I am connected to the most powerful force on Earth. This really keeps me keep going and pursuing my dreams. I like to experiment and try new tactics to connect with God and make myself aware of how Jesus lived his life and died for humanity. I look at Jesus as a person and try to imitate his life because he was sinless and lived with a defined purpose like I want to do.

Jesus has become the most influential figure in my life, and he has led me on a path that no one else can copy. He performed miracles for people, changed people's lives to this day, led a life of purpose and discipline, and biggest of all, he lived without fear of death or anything else. The fact that we still read the Bible two thousand years later is an absolutely amazing legacy one man left. How inspiring! So look to your creator as a wise mentor, and ask for guidance thirty minutes a day.

SECTION GEMS:
1. *Set a time aside to pray and learn.*
2. *Create a schedule you can stick with spiritually.*
3. *Live your life like a leader.*

Ticktock

As you have probably begun to realize, everything does not change overnight like you most likely want it to. The best success comes in increments every day. You see, my friends, great success only emerges from trials and tribulations and long years of dedication and persistence toward a goal. Most people are always looking for shortcuts to success, when frankly, this will only waste their time and cut them short of success. God's miracles and work take time to flourish. It is like planting a field of crops and waiting for the seeds to reach their full potential. It takes time for the crops to produce delicious fruit; the same is true for your life. Once you start investing time with your creator and top-notch friends, you will start to sow seeds of greatness that will eventually come to fruition when the creator says it is the correct time in your life to reap the benefits. Give time for your creator to work, and stop expecting immediate results. Start depending on him once you pray that he takes control of the situation.

SECTION GEMS:
1. *There are no shortcuts to success.*
2. *Sow the seeds for the creator to work with.*
3. *Reap the rewards when God wants you to.*
4. *Success takes time.*
5. *The creator has a plan that you can't comprehend.*

PRINCIPLE 8:
Become a Walking, Talking Charity

The Law of Giving and Receiving

Learn to give. Giving is one of the best perks of being alive. If you give in every category of life, you will be happy, I guarantee you. There is a law in the universe called the law of giving and receiving. This law states that once you give something, whether it is time, money, or effort, you will receive something back ten times the amount you gave. For example, if you volunteer at a hospital to help kids with cancer, that will in turn come back to you tenfold in multiple areas of life. Giving money provides a great example of how the law of giving and receiving works. Let us say you give one hundred dollars to a charity of your choice. Over time, you would receive an abundance of cash: one thousand dollars.

The more creative you get with giving, the more fun it will be for you and other people. Once you know you are making money to help other people survive and know that your services for others spring from love and directly correlate with your success, you will push to diversify your giving into multiple platforms.

Unfortunately, many people do not give because they do not believe their income is big enough, they are penny pinchers, and because they do not believe giving to others is worthwhile. These are all bad excuses. Even if you are the most broke person in the world, you can still give your time and effort. Taking action will not only make this world a better place, it will also give you something to do during your day, allow you to help other people, and might allow you to meet a person who could hire you or change your life.

Myles Berrio is a fantastic example of a person in my life who has become an avid giver in a very creative way. He has created a nonprofit project called Live-MoreTheHomeless, which is focused on getting people all over the world to put together bags of goodies for the homeless. They assemble bags of essentials like toothpaste, shampoo, food, candy, a Bible quote for hope, and other items. This simple gift can cost you anywhere around five dollars per bag to contribute to, and it might literally change someone's life out there on the streets. So get creative and have fun in the process.

When you give out of love and not just to gain more in life, you will be blessed. True love is the key to the equation of giving and receiving. Most people think the world is a place of greed and lust, but really it can be a lot more than that. Becoming a walking, talking charity in everything you do will help you become a person who is here to live for a legacy to change others' lives rather than living to make a paycheck every two weeks. Are you living a life of compassion or a life of selfishness? If you are living a comfortable lifestyle, you are not alone because most people are interested in that kind of idea of life. Instead of making money for just yourself, hold yourself to a higher standard and make it your obligation to go forward to dominate in your area of work to make more money for the people who NEED the extra love and cash to survive. Hold yourself to a higher standard in all areas of life and never act like the world owes you anything.

Almost all the richest people in the world are philanthropists. Is it weird that they are the most giving? Recently, I heard that Bill Gates and his wife plan to give eighty-five billion dollars to charities around the world after they have passed away. At the time of this writing, Bill Gates is worth eighty-six billion dollars, so to give eighty-five billion dollars is truly a great legacy to leave.

Most people think that a person who makes big money is obligated to use their hard-earned cash to solve other people's problems. This mindset is very poor because it is not open to the idea that the poor person needs to get more involved in giving to become more prosperous in their own lives. Again, we all can—and should—give.

> **SECTION GEMS:**
> *1. To receive, you must master giving.*
> *2. Get creative with your giving.*
> *3. Have fun with your giving.*
> *4. Give out of love.*
> *5. Break out of the poverty mentality.*
> *6. Giving correlates with success.*

Fear of Loss

One of the main fears people face regarding giving is the fear of loss. From a young age, our society convinces us that there is not enough of anything in the world to go around for everybody. I mean for goodness sake, in economics we learn that the world's resources are scarce. They try to convince us that society needs people to lose so that there can be winners. But listen to me: Everybody can win! There is enough success to go around for everybody! This limiting mindset that not everybody can win must be stopped. This, my friends, is a main reason people hesitate to give their most valuable resources: money, time, and effort. To break out of this paradigm, take a leap of faith and apply some willpower to take action. Once you see the smile on someone's face and what something like a bag of goodies can do for them, you will truly understand what it means to give with love.

SECTION GEMS:
1. *Stop fearing giving.*
2. *Break out of the scarcity mindset.*
3. *You will be prosperous through giving.*
4. *Take a leap of faith and give.*

Impact

The impact you can have on someone's life by giving to them is unbelievable. The legacy that can be left by giving is so huge if you end up doing it for the right reasons. Love is the main reason why giving can have such a large impact. And just think of it, donating money out of love, for example, could end up buying the necessary tools to allow someone to survive in a foreign country. How cool is that?! Giving goes so much further than just money. Whatever you think your purpose is on Earth, being able to give at any moment in any type of way is a luxury. Once you start spending time with people who need someone in their life, you will start to see what life is all about. After you die, you will only be remembered by the people whose lives you have touched.

Giving is a unique way to touch someone's heart and life. It is so true that not everything can go with you when you die, but they missed one thing: They forgot to add, "You can take the amount of impact, love, and amazing relationships you had with people." The whole reason we are on Earth is to love each other and always give to one another. A true legacy and impact are left when future generations tell stories about you. This major tip is so vital to success that it must never be ignored. Someone could always use something, somewhere. With every decision you make in life, you impact something in some type of way. You design your world.

SECTION GEMS:
1. *Giving leaves a footprint.*
2. *When you die, you will be remembered by the people you helped.*
3. *Every decision you make has an impact.*

31

PRINCIPLE 9:

Freedom

The Pursuit of Freedom

Freedom is one of the most misunderstood words in the world. The first step to defining freedom is to look it up in the dictionary. The definition of freedom, according to Google, is that everyone's definition of freedom is different than everybody else's. My definition of freedom might be to do what I want, when I want, and with whom I want. Your definition of freedom might be to get citizenship in a country somewhere. Whoever you are, true freedom is doing whatever you love to do, every day, no matter what. We should all be able to agree on that.

In whatever life scenario, it is strictly your choice whether you have freedom. Once you decide to pursue what you love for the rest of your life, you will be free. Let us say, for example, that your passion is working on exotic cars. If you have not grown up financially capable to see or touch an exotic car every day, then you must ensure your mind is right for the trials and tribulations that will come. Everything starts with your mindset and whether you think you are worthy to be able to own or work on exotic cars. The law of association plays a large role in this journey to get to where you want to be. There will always be naysayers along the road to your freedom. Just remember that most of them are saying bad things to you because they are jealous that you are pursuing your dream and they want you to stay at their level. Even your closest friends and family will try to hold you down sometimes. Do not let them.

When I say your dream all comes down to how bad you want it, it really is in your hands, even if it does not feel like it. Your desire to gain your freedom determines who you will try to meet and connect with, how well you will know the ins and outs of the cars, and how you will not let others' opinions stand in your way. Your passion should be something you chase the rest of your life and will make you happy until the day you die.

Another key to this journey is to find out what you want to pursue at the earliest age you can. The time you put toward your craft will highly affect your skillset and your mindset. It is costlier to start with your passion later than sooner due to obligations like taxes, paying for insurance, supporting a family, and on and on. When you are young, you typically have a lot less serious obligations and more freedom with your time. Take advantage of being young. So many people are caught up as a teenager in the traps of partying, trying to fit in, going to college, joining a fraternity or sorority, and many more things. If you truly do want to have freedom through your passion, then take every chance you get to put time toward it.

As young people, we are so convinced that we must party to fit in; but this is a major downfall in most people's lives. Teenagers start to procrastinate on their dreams of success, if they ever had any, and put their dreams off till later when serious obligations start to set in. People never reach their childhood dreams because they spend their first twenty years focused on school, friends, family, nine-to-five jobs, partying, social media, and trying to fit in. Therefore, we are molded into the mindset that we can have fun for our first twenty years and work our next forty to sixty years in hopes of being able to retire one day.

You call that freedom? Freedom is being able to go anywhere, anytime, without any obligations to anything. Once you are tied down to something, your freedom is limited. You have the choice to decide whether you will have freedom. Some outside circumstances may constrain you, but you are basically free to decide whether you are willing to pursue what you love.

SECTION GEMS:
1. *Freedom means no obligations.*
2. *Passion can be your freedom.*
3. *Escape the status quo.*
4. *Work when you are young for a playful life the rest of your life.*
5. *Follow your heart.*

Financial Freedom

Regardless of who you are, everybody needs money. Some people absolutely hate to talk about money because it makes them feel insecure about their own lives and lack of abundance. Money can allow you to be free, to do what you want, when you want, where you want, and with whom you want. Financial freedom allows people to become better givers, better lovers, better people, and better caretakers. Money and financial freedom are lacking in so many people's lives because people do not understand money. Money is not taught in school, and for some people money is not a priority because they are focused on the moment and not on the future. IT IS A NECESSITY TO BECOME FINANCIALLY SUCCESSFUL.

Whether you like money, you must have it to live. Becoming a multimillionaire takes the process of all the previous chapters and what they were about. Make money a priority, and you will experience unlimited freedoms that not only you can enjoy, but all the people in your family can enjoy, including your parents, children, husband, and wife. These freedoms can include traveling, a great education for your children, never looking at a bill again, giving at any moment to a person in need, always being able to provide for your family, and mentoring others. I started posting on Snapchat a tip of the day for one hundred days straight, and I could not believe my friends' and followers' reactions! People absolutely loved it. These tips of the day posts allowed people to see why a financially successful life could benefit them. Fans and friends started inboxing me on Snapchat and texting me about their business startup ideas and how to become successful.

Money opens almost any door in this world, and that is why you should make it your obligation to make BIG money and never settle. Buying a house and having to stay in that house for forty years is not freedom. Lack of money causes a lack of freedom. So how do we tie this section into the section before this one on passion and freedom? Once you start figuring out how to be the best at your passion and make it a priority, you will start to be noticed in that area of expertise and be paid what you are worth.

Your value is based on what you bring to the marketplace. Every area of expertise pays differently. If you are the best golfer in the world, then you are bringing huge value to the marketplace as a human advertisement for companies—on top of all the tournaments you already win. Companies will pay you big money to wear their logo or their clothes. The extremely competitive golf world has a large audience, so it generates great income.

Your passion takes time to perfect, as does your bank account. So every passion should come with a motivating factor besides money. For the longest time, you will not be making the green stuff. For some of the richest people in the world, the factor besides money seems to be creativity and always wanting to create more content for their legacy and to help as many people as they can. Money should be your end goal along with impacting others' lives, but keep multiple motivating factors in front of you so that when the money is not coming in, you will have a reason to keep pursuing your dream.

Learn about money. It is not the root of all evil. People who tell you that are broke and feel bad for themselves. Money can be used for good or evil. It all depends on your motives. To become a master of money, learn from the people who make it. It would be just like watching Michael Jordan play and looking for tips on how to be the best at basketball. Once you start building wealth and maintaining it, you can take care of many of life's difficulties.

The largest step to becoming financially successful is investing. Investing comes in many different shapes and colors. You can invest in pretty much everything: stocks, bonds, real estate, yourself, athletes, cars, and on and on. Every person who has become extremely wealthy has been an investor in something. If you learn how to invest in things that produce large returns like real estate multi-family (apartments), you will start to produce large residual income all the time. There are some common misconceptions with investing. These five misconceptions are:

1. Invest to make a little money.
2. Start investing as soon as you can.
3. "Investing is risky."
4. Diversify your portfolio.
5. Pinch pennies.

The first misconception is very important to understand and change. No one should invest to make a little bit of money. You should invest to get SUPER RICH. I mean, why would you not? The media, family, friends, and many more sources hammer people with the idea that it is best to stay inside one's comfort zone. Invest in the long haul, or invest short term if you can make a crap ton of money and know what a good deal is. But know this: If you do not study what you are investing in, there is no point of investing. It takes time to study and learn what a good deal is. If you are putting all your money on the line, why would you not want to know if you are guaranteed success?

Instead of investing your money incrementally and making small gains and experiencing small losses, invest in BIG deals to make BIG gains in cash flow. The goal is to get SUPER RICH, right? The second common misconception with investing is something I struggled with. When I was around sixteen I learned that I must start investing a lot to make significant gains in my wealth. I started too early. I was not taught that I should save my money and then put a large amount into a single investment the first time. The more you invest, the more gain comes out of it if you choose the right investment. Stocks, for example, yield small returns for the long term if you only have fifteen hundred dollars in one account. Your gains will be dollars compared to putting in three million dollars in the stock market and earning thousands of dollars in a day.

I want to tie this misconception in with misconception number three. There are so many naysayers who say, "Do not invest; it is too risky." This misconception has convinced people to never invest, or they have invested and been burned so bad that they hold a grudge against investing for the rest of their lives and on top of that, they tell other people that all investing is bad. Everything you do holds some type of risk. There is something called risk/reward. Risk/reward is a ratio that can be figured out by looking at the positives and the negatives in the investment. Do the research, and the risk will go down. The bigger the investment, the smaller the risk, the larger the reward is. An investment is only as risky as the person's knowledge and experience about that particular investment.

Start investing when you see a great investment. Do not rush into it. Also, let us clarify another important point about investing: how much you should save. If you have under one hundred thousand dollars to invest, do not invest. I repeat, do not invest if you have under one hundred thousand dollars to invest IN CASH. You can get leverage, which is borrowed funds, for an investment, but only get leverage when you know your investment can pay off your loan by itself. For example, if you have a multifamily property that costs four hundred thousand dollars, you can put down one hundred thousand dollars in cash and finance the rest. Your multifamily investment has renters. Renters pay you rent because you own the property. Guess what you can do with that rent money? Pay off the debt. Simple, right? Not for most people, unfortunately. So many people are undisciplined with their money. In multifamily investments, renters will pay off your debt until it is all gone and you can own that four-hundred-thousand-dollar property with only one hundred thousand dollars down. Talk about big gains! Before buying something that large though, you must know it is a GREAT deal. Remember it is only risky if you make it risky by diving into an investment you have no idea about.

The fourth misconception about investments is that you must diversify your money into a lot of investments to stay safe. This is the most misunderstood misconception of them all. I myself was taught from a very young age to diversify my portfolio in investing to "spread my risk." But every successful person has stuck to a single investment and run with it. Thank goodness I finally understand this. I had been trying to have a hand in everything. I had wanted to be the best at real estate, a social media expert, videographer, and the best author. After talking with my friend James White, an amazing golfer who was ranked seven in the world as an amateur, I realized I needed to stop spreading myself so thin and start pursuing the one craft that was my passion. I thank God every day for allowing me to hear what James had to say and for applying his advice in my life.

Your investment does not have to be financial. Apply all your pressure to a single craft and dominate that sector. The richest and most successful people in the world became experts in their own specific fields before they ever started diving into other fields of professionalism. The cast of the TV show *Shark Tank*—Mark Cuban, Kevin O'Leary, Barbara Corcoran, Daymond John, Robert Herjavec, and Lori Greiner—are fantastic examples of investors who perfected their craft and then moved on to invest money earned off their craft into other businesses that walk into the "tank." You might say, "Well, in *Shark Tank*, the sharks are diversifying their investments into different companies." They might be, but they have so much money to invest that a small investment for them of one hundred thousand dollars might end up producing a million dollars. Also notice that they a) only invest if they know something is a great investment, b) feel like they can help that person in that business, and c) believe the owner is not extremely overpricing the company.

The fifth and final misconception is a very powerful concept to learn: Stop penny pinching at every opportunity. I grew up with the penny pinching paradigm, but recently broke out of it—thank God! Take your focus off saving and start focusing on producing! No one has ever gotten rich from saving and penny pinching. Be on offense! You should be on offense 90 percent of the time and defense, saving, 10 percent of the time. Overall, financial prosperity should be made an obligation and not something to ignore and put to the side.

SECTION GEMS:
1. *Make financial success a necessity.*
2. *Invest to become SUPER RICH.*
3. *Avoid the misconceptions of investing.*
4. *Specialize. Do not diversify.*
5. *Wealth equals freedom.*
6. *Producing > penny pinching.*

PRINCIPLE 10:
Venturing into the Unknown

Comfort Zone

When is the last time you did something that scared you? Everything you could ever want is outside of your comfort zone. Are you willing to take the necessary steps to get what you want, or are you going to cave back into your comfort zone? The decision is up to you.

Below is a visual perception of what the comfort zone looks like. In your head, you have something called a brain, hopefully. It is a muscle you can train. A part of your brain controls your "limits." These limits are your comfort zone. Just like any other body part, you can train this part of your brain to be tougher and stronger willed so that you can stop getting stuck due to your unwillingness to step outside of your comfort zone. The secret to getting out of the zone is something you already know to do but do not want to do: Keep doing things that are outside of your comfort zone. If you are in sales and have to make cold calls every once in a while or every day, you know the pressure you face on that first call. If you are slightly introverted, you will feel nervous going out of your comfort zone on that first, second, third, and fourth call. Move past the little

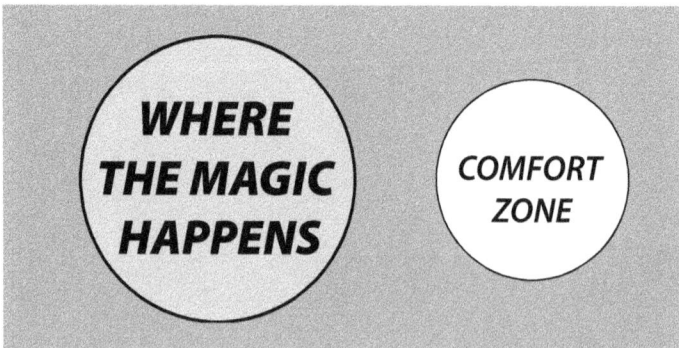

WHERE THE MAGIC HAPPENS

COMFORT ZONE

voices in your head and attack. Frequency is more important than perfection. Once you start making a bunch of calls, cold calling will become part of your comfort zone and no response will ever surprise you. The more calls you make, the greater chance someone will pick up the phone and buy or sell.

Consistency and frequency are the keys to killing the fear of failure. It would be the same as asking a hot girl or guy out. It is all a numbers game and all in the confidence to take the first step to execute getting out of your comfort zone. We are so persuaded to stay where we are and never proceed past where we feel comfortable. The enemy of abundance is comfort. So the thing that is holding you back from this success is YOU and YOU only. It is all in your head. Abundance is destined for you only if you decide to act.

SECTION GEMS:
1. *Everything you want is outside of your comfort zone.*
2. *Consistency is the key to killing fear.*
3. *Dominate where others will not venture.*

Conclusion

Whatever obstacle you face, just know that you are powerful beyond belief. Start to apply these ten principles, and you will see results. Give them time to work. Victory and greatness are upon you. I hope for the best for you, your life, and your family.

10 Principle Checklist

- ☐ I am pursuing my purpose, passion, and legacy.
- ☐ I believe I am the one.
- ☐ I have set all my daily goals.
- ☐ I have set weekly goals.
- ☐ I have set monthly goals.
- ☐ I have set yearly goals.
- ☐ I have set goals in increments of 5 and 10 years.
- ☐ I have a positive mentor in my life.
- ☐ I have 5 positive influences in my life.
- ☐ I have assembled a mastermind alliance.
- ☐ I am immersed in my craft every day.
- ☐ I am taking in personal development every day.
- ☐ I focus on the positives in every situation.
- ☐ I work a minimum of 10 hours a day toward my passion and goals.
- ☐ I enjoy working every day.
- ☐ I pray and ask for help every day.
- ☐ I know my worth is determined by what God says about me and not what people say about me.
- ☐ I have strong faith, and I am destined for greatness.
- ☐ I understand that I must give in order to receive.
- ☐ I actively give my time and money to people in need.
- ☐ I love everybody no matter what they have done to me.
- ☐ I am going to make an impact on Earth.
- ☐ I am confident in my ability to perform.
- ☐ I am making it my obligation to chase freedom.
- ☐ I am making it my obligation to chase financial freedom and become SUPER RICH.
- ☐ I am not afraid to fight for freedom to do what I want, when I want, with whom I want.
- ☐ I have gone outside my comfort zone at least once today.
- ☐ I am making it my obligation to remove the chains of worry, stress, and anxiety by stepping outside of my comfort zone.

www.ingramcontent.com/pod-product-compliance
Lightning Source LLC
Chambersburg PA
CBHW022345040426
42449CB00006B/734